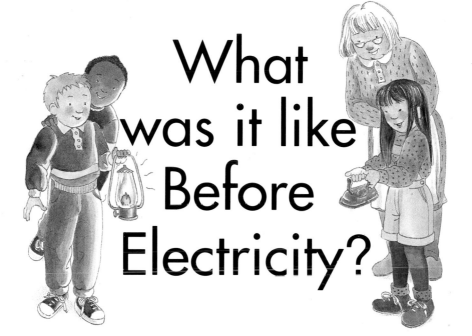

# What was it like Before Electricity?

Paul Bennett

*Illustrated by*
Carolyn Scrace

4

Her house is really interesting with lots of old stuff in it.

The house is so old. It was built before there was electricity. There are still the old gas lamps on the wall. Can you see them?

Show us around the house, Great-grandma.

6

We want to see all the old junk.

It's not old junk. There are lots of old memories here. Come with me and I'll tell you about some of them.

When I was a girl we used oil lamps
because there were no electric lights.
I went to bed by candlelight.

*That must have been spooky!*

That's not a tennis racket. It's a carpet beater. When I was younger there were no machines to clean carpets.

I had to hang our carpets on a washing line and beat them with that. I got very dusty I can tell you.

I bet it's easier now you've got a vacuum cleaner!

Nearly every room had a fireplace.
We burned wood or coal to keep
warm. We did all our cooking on
a wood or coal stove, too.

Sometimes we would use a paraffin
heater. You filled the tank at the bottom
with paraffin and then lit the wick. Our
house always smelled of paraffin.

Well, you see that old tub over there? That was our wash tub. Every Monday, my mother used to wash all the clothes by hand.

The water was heated over a coal fire. She stirred the clothes with a wooden paddle, called a dolly.

*That sounds like hard work to me!*

Then she squeezed the clothes through
the thing with the two rollers over there.
It's called a mangle. If you got your
fingers caught in it, you knew it!

She hung the clothes on the line or by the fire to dry. Our house was always full of wet washing.

They are flat irons. We had to heat them up on top of a coal stove. My mother would spit on them to see if they were hot.

Television hadn't been invented
when I was your age. After school I
used to play hopscotch or roll a
wooden hoop. Here's an old one.

They are flat irons. We had to heat them up on top of a coal stove. My mother would spit on them to see if they were hot.

*Hey! Look at this funny old record player!*

That's my gramophone. I used to play music on that and dance to it when I was a child.

You had to wind it up. That trumpet thing makes the sound. I've still got some old records somewhere. We could try it.

Can I wind it up?

Television hadn't been invented
when I was your age. After school I
used to play hopscotch or roll a
wooden hoop. Here's an old one.

In the evening I would play the violin
or the piano, or read a book.

I had a doll with a china head. Of course, we didn't have any battery-powered toys.

My brother had some clockwork toys and we both liked to play marbles.

Well, trains were very different in my day. When I was a girl we used to travel by steam train. They were very noisy and dirty.

Clouds of smoke came billowing out of the funnel as we chugged along.

Yes, it has made my life easier, but
we still had good times in those days.

Can you name the things on this page? The answers are at the bottom of the page but don't peep until you have tried yourself.

30